Cats

Gerald and Julie Hawksley

Consultant: Dr. Stanley J. Truffini, DVM

MALLARD
PRESS

This edition published by Mallard Press, an imprint of BDD
Promotional Book Company, Inc., 666 Fifth Avenue, New York,
New York 10103. Mallard Press and its accompanying design
and logo are trademarks of BDD Promotional Book Company, Inc.

Contents

Your Cat

Pet cats belong to the same family as lions and tigers. Like these wild cats they are carnivores, which means that they eat meat.

Cats like to hunt, but they don't usually chase their prey. Instead they creep up to it and pounce. Pet cats like to do this with toys such as balls and crumpled pieces of paper.

Cats can be let outdoors on their own, but you should keep an eye on them. They can be kept indoors if you live in an apartment.

You should never buy a cat unless you have the time to feed it regularly and give it a loving, caring home.

Types of Cats

Most pet cats are a mixture of lots of different types. They can be all sorts of colors, with long or short fur. They make good, loving pets.

Tortoiseshells have black, light red and dark red patches of fur.

Tabbies have striped coats, with darker markings on a light background. They can be gray, brown or orange.

Black cats are traditionally believed to bring bad luck.

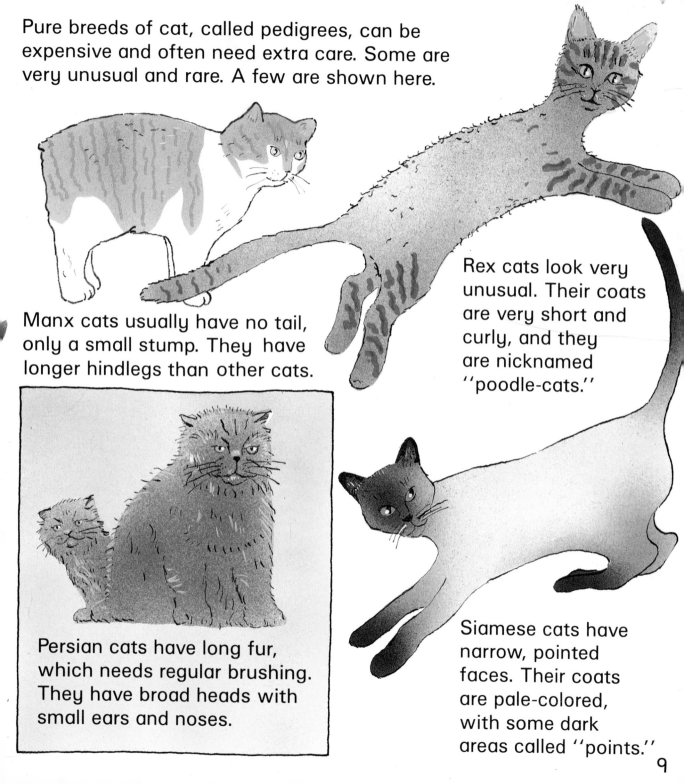

Pure breeds of cat, called pedigrees, can be expensive and often need extra care. Some are very unusual and rare. A few are shown here.

Manx cats usually have no tail, only a small stump. They have longer hindlegs than other cats.

Rex cats look very unusual. Their coats are very short and curly, and they are nicknamed "poodle-cats."

Persian cats have long fur, which needs regular brushing. They have broad heads with small ears and noses.

Siamese cats have narrow, pointed faces. Their coats are pale-colored, with some dark areas called "points."

9

Things You Need

You will need something safe to carry your new pet home in. Use a secure box or a pet basket.

Cats need a litter box indoors. Put it in a quiet place away from food bowls. You may want to line it with newspaper before filling it with litter.

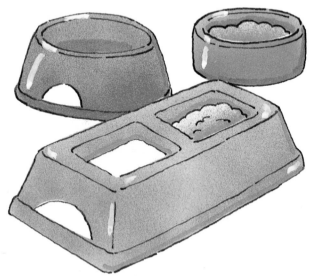

Your cat will need shallow, sturdy food and water bowls that won't tip over.

**Box lined
with a blanket**

Pet basket

Large, soft pillow

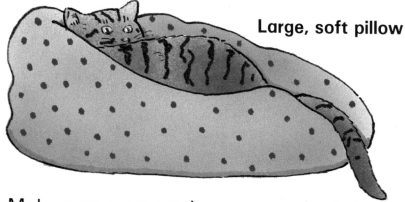

Make sure your cat has a warm bed. A kitten will be happy with a box that is lined and cut down. This will help your kitten climb in and out. Later on get a basket or a large, soft pillow.

Get your cat a collar and a tag with your name and address on it.

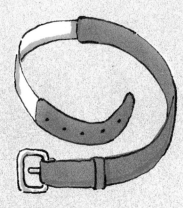

Elastic collars are best because cats can wriggle out of them if they get caught on a branch or a bush.

Kittens

When you get a new kitten, put out some food and water and show your pet its bed and litter box. It will take some time for your kitten to get used to its new home. Don't take a kitten away from its mother until it is 7 or 8 weeks old.

When you pick a kitten up use both hands, and don't hold it too tightly. Never pick a kitten up by the scruff of its neck.

When your kitten is eight weeks old take it to the vet for a checkup and some vaccinations to protect it against illnesses.

Kittens over a month old will need four or five small meals a day. You can buy nourishing canned food especially for them. Make sure you put out water, too.

Kittens love to play, so give your kitten plenty of toys, such as balls of yarn, empty spools and crumpled pieces of paper.

Mealtime

Kittens gradually need fewer meals as they get older. Cats over nine months old need two or three small meals a day. Give your pet a varied diet of canned food. Use a small amount of dried food as well, because crunching it is good for your cat's teeth.

Cats like to be fed at the same time each day. They don't usually eat food all at once, but come back to it later.

Cats usually drink some water while they are outside, but always make sure that your cat has fresh water to drink indoors.

It is best to keep food from an opened can in a plastic container in the refrigerator.

Cats at Home

Dogs usually get along with cats when they share a home, but if you have any small pets, such as hamsters or mice, put their cages well out of reach of your cat.

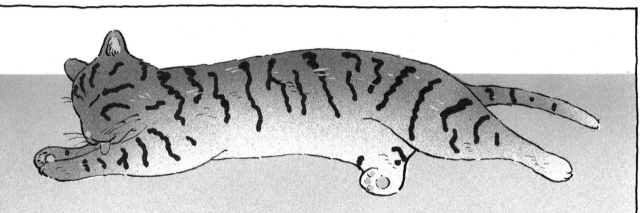

Cats are very clean animals and take great care washing themselves. They are usually easy to housebreak and will learn to use their litter tray quickly. If you put your pet in its litter tray after every meal, it will soon go there on its own.

Older cats like to keep their claws healthy and sharp by scratching at things. If your yard doesn't have trees or fences, or your pet lives indoors all the time, you should get a scratching post or a small log.

Your cat will growl in anger at a strange cat or purr with pleasure when you pet it. It will meow to go out or to ask for food.

Healthy Cats

Always keep a check on your cat's health, and if you think it is ill ask a grown-up to help you take it to a vet.

You should get your cat spayed or neutered by a vet as soon as possible, to stop a female cat from having kittens and a male cat from wandering away from home.

It is important to brush long-haired cats daily, because their fur can tangle easily.

If your cat has short hair brush it once or twice a week to keep its coat shiny and to get rid of loose hair. You should brush more often when cats are molting, which is when they lose lots of fur.

Your cat may pick up fleas, so regularly dust its coat with flea powder. You can also buy collars which keep fleas away.

Grooming is a good time to check that your cat's teeth and ears are clean, and that its claws aren't too long. A vet can show you how to trim the claws.

If you take good care of your cat it will stay fit and healthy. Make sure you give it lots of love and attention.

Out and About

Cats like to spend a lot of their day outside, especially when the weather is warm.

Wait until your cat is used to its new home before letting it outdoors. A kitten can go out after it has had its first vaccinations.

You could ask someone to fit a pet door to the back door so your cat can go in and out.

Once your cat begins to explore outdoors it will meet other neighborhood cats. The first meetings may be noisy and unfriendly, but after a while your cat will be accepted.

Cats are safer indoors at night, especially in cities with busy roads.

If you go away, make sure your pet is well cared for by a friend or neighbor, or board your cat in a good local kennel.

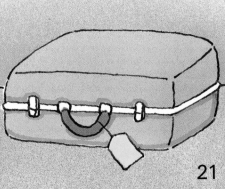

Do's and Don'ts

Here are some of the most important things to remember:

★ **Do** go to a local home for unwanted cats if you are looking for a new pet. You will find lots of cats and kittens who need good homes.

★ **Do** keep new cats indoors for a week or two, until they get to know you and their new home. After a while you can start to put them outside just before meals. They will soon come back if they are hungry.

★ **Do** go and see your vet if you do not want a female cat to have lots of kittens, or a male cat to wander away from home a lot, or get into fights. The vet will do a harmless operation to neuter or spay your pet.

★ **Do** pick up and hold your cat properly — with one hand firmly underneath its back legs. It will feel safer and more comfortable if you do this.

★ **Do** put your cat's litter box in a quiet, private place, away from any food bowls.

★ **Don't** feed your cat too much, or it will become fat and unhealthy.

★ **Don't** neglect your cat and expect it to look after itself. Cats have an independent nature, but they like company and need care like any other pet.

★ **Don't** give your cat any medication unless you have checked with a vet first.